Riding Bareback
Backwards

Riding Bareback Backwards

poems by
Christina Quinn

Poetic Justice Books & Arts
Port Saint Lucie, Florida

©2019 Christina Quinn

book design and layout: SpiNDec, Port Saint Lucie, FL
cover image: *Horse*, Christina Quinn

All rights reserved.

No part of this book may be used or reproduced in any manner whatsoever without written permission except in the case of brief quotations embodied in critical articles and reviews. Members of educational institutions and organizations wishing to photocopy any of the work for classroom use, or authors, artists and publishers who would like to obtain permission for any material in the work, should contact the publisher.

Published by Poetic Justice Books
Port Saint Lucie, Florida
www.poeticjusticebooks.com

ISBN: 978-1-950433-14-8

FIRST EDITION
10 9 8 7 6 5 4 3 2 1

Riding Bareback Backwards

here inside this empty
this insulate
I crave my life in encapsulated linear equation
worked & reworked
as if there could be any other outcome
—
he erases indelible & leaves roughened paper smudges
like proof of life or someone she once was
—
i am grateful for those histories i don't own
grateful for the distance of years
if only to be free from the sin
indelibly printed in my bones
i am a fascinated horror
the succubus of dreams
i count their names & weigh the balance
i don't know who i am

weather surrounds us like a love story
a ripped bodice lust of smutty paperbacks
we vie for the circular dryness of cheap umbrellas
inside
a struggle out of damp jackets
damp boots
damp damp hair
shaking stringed raindrops into dry space
rain sluices across the too orange cedar stained deck
leaving crystalline pools on the wooden surface
so recently hammered & sawn by Sy & Jimmi
in short days of too much sun
too much beer
—
this was all before you, dog, i say
still, you'd like him if he were here
you'd like him
until the wriggle of bed & blankets
the gentle heave of warm breath
& the cold nose of love

It's a civil war like permanent winter
still at night the sky dresses up in drag
a myriad of stars
frost encrusted
all a sparkle
rain comes in soft & slow &
then with dismembering intensity
holy jesus i think
let's make water into wine
put out catchment barrels &
sell drinks by the side of highway 74
one swig will save you
have you walking on water
& in the interests of civic duty
i will confiscate your car keys
because you know
the winding road
leading down down down
into the hell of snowbird heaven

the bartender spins glass over terry toweled clean
more & many glass shelves behind
cluttered with colored
—

like soldiers ain't they he gleams
—

my teeth ache
but the
no never mind inside thought begins
the bartender shrugs
—

its in yer 'ands in it love
glass eyes drip adoration

its mostly nights
but sometimes
on nondescript days
you perch on the edge of my mind
tapping that damn ball point pen against
the turned up brim of your monday hat
& because the day reveals nothing of interest
i allow myself to sit
beneath pink bougainvillea flourish
a notepad & pen resting atop a metal table
battling the faraway look in your eye
& from the toweled sag of ancient whicker
i shade the sun from my eyes
& think of the craziness of loving
of writing
of painting almost
in the sly way of two perfect cats with perfect toes
slinking among the shadows of pink petals
but mostly i listen
to unseen neighbors &
the sweet syncopate of shared music
drifting over walls covered in pink bougainvillea
flourish

wouldn't it be nice to make new friends
as dogs do
tip to tail
noses up butts
getting the shit & piss out of the way
in great snorting huffs

you are still
the one who makes me smile
still the black to my white
jazz to my blues
the fruit to my loop
&
under pages & pages written &
the intentional slaps of commaless realities
you are still making love to my mind
i see what you did
((parentheses parentheses))
she ends on a high note
@alright then he sez

i made the bed before i left
i plumped up pillows
turned down the sheets
just in case thieves break in
& maybe like goldilocks
they'd be distracted by
the invitation of crisp clean sheets
perhaps lie there & leaf through books or watch
andy goldsworthy making twigs talk art on the vcr
refreshed they'd leave to rob other someones
who have left beds unmade
& i'd return to find
a faint impression of
goldilocks on my sheets

we're sort of freaks really
if i need to demonstrate how & where
i just might be trying to beguile you
what if we just revel
in the oddities of who we are
repetitions of one kind or another
make for shakes of head & heart
but if you really need to know
i met someone who speaks volumes
he's stuck inside my head
& i'm compelled to impress
it's protocol so
let the clinical study begin
sooner or later
aren't we all turned inside out &
the truth in our heads never stops
next time you should walk
but not like that i say
not alone

one step in the wrong direction &
the resulting blue
a suggested privilege
such a disastrous assumption considering
the truth &
for some mad reason
it's been fascinating
perception versus reality
as if we are all pre-programmed
to choose stripes instead of spots
dear reader
it's a mathematical equation
over which we have no control
patterns will form regardless
it's a beautiful feature of life
watching the leopard grow
counting his spots
& until i look in the mirror
my eyes might just as well
have been brown

i'm taking out the trash
...
heaviest thing he said all day
...
not to be taken lightly
this domestic masking of unspoken
of truth waiting at the pearly gates
sunshine making here & now
bugs all a pest at the stink of three day trash
—
i turn away
nose held
—
is this the end? i ask
no
he replies

she takes a moment
to make an aside
—
she talks too much
realizations fall thick & fast
the world shimmers in white gleam
reminiscent of fresh snowfalls
underneath the longing is
too hot & waiting to explode
a further aside
because
she is captured
enraptured & heaves
a patently obvious sigh
blowing through dreams
like green green leaves in shuddered touch
tossing feel goods all over the pavement
really
all over the paving

sometimes the smell of sulfurstruck tobacco
lit but not yet inhaled smoke
comes to me in a dream
sometimes the taste of golden virginia
perfectly spread across white glue tipped zig zag teases my tongue
sometimes the sight of a perfectly rolled smoke
not too tight or moist
a burner an easy puff
a sweet curled tongue thrust of smoke
&
sometimes the dream comes with ice cold
lime salted tecate
as if they are conjoined twins
welded in right handed can & grasped two finger toke
& i want them in the way of long lost lovers &
remembered lust

it might rain directly he said
looking up
—

under his shadow a stink bug scuttles
grounded on parchment
behind them an orchard of windmills
wings clipped by lost breezes are
still waiting for a first drop
a slim gust makes passage
arms shudder & groan
—

it's a slow turn of events for windmills
& old men with petrified bones
—

between heavy drops & near misses
he waits
face turned up

if you don't mind
i'll be a cell phone tower
pinging & popping with far off words
beaming in from india or oman
promising a wealth of riches
—
i'll be the spin of 78 rpms
a needled skip & hiss floating peggy lee or eartha kitt
out the window
down to the corner of jackson & 111 where the homeless guy
taps feet & waves his cardboard sign at somnambulant motorists
—
i'll be a plastic bag skipping over traffic playing sudden death with
tractor trailers blocking all three lanes &
swirling in the breeze of passing freight
—
yet here i am
i painted the room
cleaned & rearranged
shopped for crisp white linens
& a lava lamp
carried acres of garbage out to the curb
rid bookshelves of nonsense &
alphabetized poets by name
& there you were
sneaking into the corners again

he owned five suits
all identical in cut & hue
only his ties colored the day
red & blue & purple striped
knotted against a background of shirts
white & freshly laundered
—
his briefcase was good brown leather
overly supple from the years
shoes brown & wing tipped
a faint mist of bay rum cologne
clouded his chin
—
he had worked hard
all his life
hours spent
selling an assortment of brushes & fuller's earth
door to door
a gig in a used car lot
& the pinnacle of his career
life insurance
pushing the security of
comfortable permanent sleep
while heirs & such reap the benefits
—
the first day of his retirement
he cleaned
he cooked
he read
& still the hours were only half filled
he stared at the clock
mulling over his choices

—
the next day he put on his suit
a clean shirt
& the blue striped tie
laced up his wingtips
grabbed his briefcase
a bag of peanuts
two bottles of water
& a map of america
he closed up the house
locking the door & windows
& set off
heading south
one measured step in front of the other
he smiled
he had all the time in the world

we sat on the balcony overlooking the sea
the sky was heavy with clouds
in the distance the sheen of rain & the spatter of
drops on water foretold of coming storms
we'd better go inside he says & slides open the door to
the room
i shrug & sip iced tecate through salt lime
come inside he says it's gonna storm soon
but we sit there all night under wind & rain
sipping beer & watching the sea climb rocks & spill
onto the rusty rail of the balcony
you're crazy he laughs
i shout into the wind
i love the ocean

early morning
streak orange blue sky
slip nose shaded eye sweat
& a fly
smaller than most
no buzz of warning
just landed uninvited
a swat
a flit from nose to brow
a blast of pursed lip air
he flies from there to here
lands on the bridge of slipped shades &
so eye to eye we circle the loop
i think
i'll call him frank
unimpressed
he leaves

i'll leave you three strawberries
three succulent berries
to stain your tongue
your teeth will sparkle white against ruby red flesh
& oh my darling
your breath will be sweet &
perfume the whisper of air that lies between us
when our mouths meet
i shall taste summer & rain &
even though there are no birds in sight
i'll hear their song & the flutter of perfect wings
i'll leave you three strawberries
three perfect red fruit
& tomorrow
tomorrow I shall leave
a handful of blue

she sits patiently
her two sons attempt to jump start her car
she waits behind the wheel
her hair in curlers
sleep still in her eyes
tethered by her boys as
they make gesture from deep under the hood
she turns the motor
the engine cranks over
it makes me think of umbilical cords
apron strings
& how we are never really disconnected

i'm touch typing in the dark
amazed
i discovered the u
i thought i touched
is really i
or is that the other way round
backspace
backspace
backspace

i saw your picture today
you looked sad
or maybe pensive
as if lines were being formed
in some strange meter like
parker & monk
well
what i really want to say is
your eyes
the right
coal black
the left reflecting
mirrored worlds
perhaps
me looking at you
looking at
me
& the thing is
well
I do
like lady
like blues

i met a corpse
on emerson boulevard
unintentional
he said & smiled in deathly array
my wheels made canyons
through his flesh
i catch the fade of his smile
but large objects
appear smaller
in hindsight

there's comfort in your snore
the rumbled inhale
the apexed silence of breath held
the gentle flip flap of exhalation
there's comfort in the hunch of your shoulder
the crowned hand arrested in dreaming flight
the weighted slump of your side of the bed
—
i try to fill the empty space
with diagonal limbs & many pillowed sprawl
the 3 a.m. tv
imitating the vibrato of you
but mostly not
the hollowed bed lays quiet
pillows mutter among themselves
missing
like me
the grumbled hitch & exhale of you

a flicker of
manic glee
the loveliness of flames
devouring dry scrub
stately pines
spewing resin
& the smell of incense above a crown of fire
he was back
fucking the night
& the night
loved him
he enjoyed every moment as if
each spark were a spasm of release
each falling branch a shudder of lust
afterwards
he smoked
& carefully
field dressed
the butt

a spoken indifference
was it all for nothing he wonders
she hums a tune behind oaken doors
& despite past disregard
a painting of fish reappears
reclaimed from behind the storage shed
they swim he says
in trees
they hang like fruit
with shimmeree of iridescent scale
& slink of magical vertebrae
she sighs &
raises blue or possibly green
depending on the scenery
flicks lids like the open & close of doors
i can save this she says
& paints until
they swim once more
weaving between leaf & willowy branches
aha he says
i see

i watch for
black raybans
you know the kind of frame
serious bookish persons wear
yet
without black electric tape holding together the broken arm
of stumbled drunken fall mishap
without the slump of nose slip slide
waiting to be pushed up from square tipped fingers
& crowned hand
without you behind the goldfish bowls
of myopic blind
the fumbled search for seeing eyes
that squint & blink of recognition when set in place
beneath bedhead hair
without all this
they are just
spectacles

starlings are bouncing
across patches of mowed grass
green squares casually strung together by
stitched concrete borders
i wonder if god is skipping starlings
as he stands street side
pleasantly bored with this uneventful day
& working up to a triple split
skipping ruffled brown birds
far off into the distance
& squinting as they disappear down 48th

he lived simply
an oracle
requiring no silver across his palm
maybe a beer or french fries from in n out
he told me i would marry a man who knew cars &
i would live well into my eighties
i laughed &
handed him a dos equis
i had two children almost grown
no intention of others
i was married to a seller of boats
& i planned on living no longer than sixty five
an optimal amount of time to see children grow
avoiding the toothless gums & rheumy eye of old old
age
—

it was the first time i heard a voice
in the parking structure across the street
the acoustics amplifying the pleasure of notes sung
purely for here it is & why not
—

several thursdays later
a tenor sax joined in
floating notes from a second floor balcony
glistening slip n slides to the croon of echoed songs
under a cloudless night
—

earthquake weather said nora
& it was
at seven forty two a.m. the structure collapsed
the balcony clung then dropped
—

three evenings of the sax man
battling the boom of boxes jabbering news in
espanol & sometimes english
three evenings of solid ground

then the earth shook again
& it was quiet
quiet
—
he should have warned me

it felt like one of those white seersucker days
a day for panama hats & aviator glasses
for umbrella'd drinks coloring white table cloths in
shades of tea or bourbon & sprigged mint
a breeze blown moisture
seeps through the head of a broken sprinkler
closed eyes turn interiors red & flesh tone
even cats tip toe
slinking through shadows cast away by melted trees
birds taking siesta
dogs laying low &
droop eyed while
flies multiply
& ants make
business
i flood dreams with escape
sailing the keys
jamaica & far off tortuga
anywhere but here

dom & me
at the oceanographic lagoon
we lunch with cannibals
in pinstriped suits
jailbreak black n white
some in sharkskin blue
busty divas flash silver lame & their bellow suck air
we don't care for the waiter they lie
only the food
& grin through human teeth with bullet eyes
a porcine squint in fleshy jest
the waiter arrives later late
as gathered congregation waits
he pulls on a purple glove
assuredly they do not eat each other
he says
& throws flecks of slivered silvered flesh
denying the fishiness of it all
they grin
through smack & huff of teeth snapped yum
& eye the waiter's purple hand

the first time i saw
that ridiculous hat
pork pie we call 'em
where i come from
& tupac being solemn
all over your shirt
ray bans hanging
tight with
black electric tape
i thought
here's another poser
about to drone on about
some inconsequential shit
but the hat reeled me in
&
you might think i'm crazy but
i'm still in love with that hat
it turns up in unexpected places
sitting quietly on park benches
browsing the poetry section at b & n
or over by the stoli stand at winco
framed in windows on downtown buses &
yep that hat makes my heart beat
fast & slow all jerk & shock
the way you used to do

it occurred to me
as we passed red cloud road
we should just keep driving
over the chiriaco summit
29 miles of long & thirsty
going who knows where
—
power lines check miles
from back to front
strung together like wire sentinels
i think of the faithful
flicking switches all their lives
with no thought just
blind belief in something
even if from who knows where
—
wind rattles the downed glass &
foot propped slouch
of too much
of last night's
whistling booze breath snores
—
i think
i don't know how far i can go
maybe this is too far
you wake in time to say
pull over
we've come too far

the invite said
office hours
—

he was there to make a sequel
others came as musicians
picture takers & makers
writers & such
making sense of in-sensibilities
—

i think of a color
indigo
on white
a kodachrome of time caught
indigo on white linen
i laugh at the silliness
of wanting to paint these moments
when all around
is the invitation
—

this ain't no rehearsal
he says
this
is
going down on film

this last child of mine
in small boy fear & curiosity
asked one day
'member when we had wings ?
i shrug my shoulders
he shrugs his

yea i said
he sighs me too

we sleep spooned & sheetless
white skin stuck to moist brown
opened windows & hoped for breezes
bring only bugs & the chain saw buzz
of hummingbird moths
drunk on evening primrose
—

in the alley out back
desert winds pluck leaves from trees
sanding away the grist of wasted
papers & plastic
clustered corners
—

a vortex of debris & sand
blows in to the yard
testing windows & doors for entrance
carelessly throwing
bougainvillea petals
through the window
a frivolous merry go round
filling spaces with shades of magenta
& tea rose pink
—

look c … its snowing i laugh
but
you sleep
unaware of the lace blanket
covering skin & sheets & books
& frosting light over sleeping cats
—

i step quiet to the window &
in amongst the pretty confusion
i scoop up armfuls & step into the night
the wind takes the offering
making pink dervishes all around

—
in the morning
you say
i dreamed you in a snow storm
all pink & petaled like summer
the cats just smile

you need to swoop me up baby
swoooop like owls under kerouac moons
—

we've reached an impasse i say
i step outside watching the sky
there is no moon
no owls
only the coo of doves
& dry heat
—

c ... i say
there's no moon out here
you smile sideways from the pillow
tonight you say
moon's gonna be here tonight
—

i look at the bottle
at the half gone
then i kiss your mouth
& the words to come

must have been up the ladder all day
diverting summer's blast through
a release of flies in the stink above yesterday's trash
I recall
in between several bouts of vertigo
flicked cigarettes trailing embers into the wake of fast cars
the smallest spark brewing the urge for conflagration
  in my tiny heart
I step down
almost as good as ginger rogers spinning end to end
her delicate footwork
i mutter delicate is as delicate does
the paving in all its radiant heat pushes scorched fingers
  through the soles of my shoes
I dwell on the smallest ember searing into the smallest toe
oh shit &
hot diggetty here comes colonel sanders
what is needed right heeyah is a damn good fire
spluttered from the corner of his moustache
he's got that shit eating grin on
he thinks it makes up for his interminable tease
& the secret recipe dribbling down his cheek
he follows behind sparking his own blend of seasoning
across the shimmer of heat
like a priest exorcising the devil
i lean the ladder against the wall
until tomorrow

in the distance of remembered lives
& for most of mine
lessons were taught by the dead & gone
dead & gone
—
hah!
those couple of close calls
left only marks
i believe in luck
& the power of silent rage
—
are you done now
can i gather the broken pieces
take them to the river

about the author

Christina Quinn is an artist and poet.
These days she resides in California.

www.ingramcontent.com/pod-product-compliance
Lightning Source LLC
Chambersburg PA
CBHW030134100526
44591CB00009B/661